This book is dedicated to all those who put in the countless hours of work
that make Joe Louis Arena the best hockey venue in the world.
Your tireless efforts and unmatched dedication
have set a standard of excellence around the National Hockey League
and made the Detroit Red Wings franchise
one of the most highly regarded and respected organizations in professional sports.

And to the fans of Hockeytown:
all of this franchise's success would not be possible without your constant support and loyalty.
Not only do you represent the greatest bunch of hockey-loving people in the world,
you hold the love of the game close to your hearts
and allow us to create memorable experiences that last a lifetime for you and your families.

Thank you~
The Detroit Red Wings

FORTY-EIGHT HOURS

with

The Detroit Red Wings

Photographed by
Steven Kovich

Text by Michael Reed

Published by Olympia Entertainment

Executive Editor: Michael Bayoff
Managing Editor: Michael Reed
Team Photographer: Steven Kovich
Art Direction: Michelle Chmura
Senior Designer: Kelly Nykanen
Copy Editor: Ann Jacobs Mooney
Editorial Assistant: Abby Heugel

Photography Credits

Cover photo by Steven Kovich
All photos by Steven Kovich except for the following:

Michael Reed - Page 1

Justin Munter - Pages 82, 83, 85, 94 (all), 102, 103 (all), 107 (top), 117 (bottom), 133 (top), 134-135, 136, 137 (all)

Mike Raffin - Pages 84, 86, 88 (inset), 91, 92, 96 (bottom), 97-100 (all), 112, 113 (top), 114, 122, 126, 127 (top), 132, 133 (bottom), 138 (all), 139

ISBN: 0-9664120-4-4

Printed in Canada

Foreword

I've been with the Red Wings organization for over 20 years now, and during that time I've seen this city and the fans at Joe Louis Arena come a long way. I remember in the early '80s when the stands were nearly empty - we would give cars away during intermissions just to attract fans to the games. Now Red Wings' tickets are the hottest in town. It's a testament to all the hard work that our owners, Mike and Marian Ilitch, have put into this franchise, along with the thousands of people that have worked in the Red Wings organization over the years.

But when you come down to watch a Red Wings' contest, or perhaps watch it on television, the hard work that goes into making each game run smoothly often gets overlooked. Although the attention is mostly on the players, it takes hundreds upon hundreds of people to make a home game at Joe Louis Arena a memorable experience.

Often before the sun rises, workers show up at the arena to take care of the little things like food preparation, setting up merchandise and making sure that the telecast that enters your home will be of the best quality.

I remember when I first started here in Detroit; there was such a small staff. But over the years we've grown into a large family that has perfected the craft of creating memorable experiences for our fans.

That's precisely why we bring this book to you. The following pages contain a look inside at what takes place behind the scenes at Joe Louis Arena. You'll follow a full day of preparation, which culminates as the Red Wings play host to the Phoenix Coyotes. From there, you'll experience all the hard work that goes into preparing the team for a road trip as you fly on Red Bird II to Columbus and watch the Red Wings take on the Blue Jackets.

The following is a bird's eye view of two days with Hockeytown's favorite team. We hope that this book not only refreshes old memories, but also creates new ones that last a lifetime.

Enjoy!

Jim Devellano
Senior Vice President/Alternate Governor
Detroit Red Wings

Contents

~ CHAPTER FOUR ~
Leaving on a Jet Plane

~ CHAPTER FIVE ~
Rise and Shine on the Road

~ CHAPTER SIX ~
Warming Up the Ice, Part II

~ CHAPTER SEVEN ~
Detroit Red Wings vs. Columbus Blue Jackets

CHAPTER ONE
Early Morning Joe

(previous page) This two-day journey alongside the Detroit Red Wings begins at the steps of Joe Louis Arena. Open since December of 1979, the Joe sits on the southern banks of the Detroit River and stands as the capitol of Hockeytown, USA.

In less than 10 hours from now, Joe Louis Arena will be transformed from this sleeping giant to a packed house with over 20,000 fans present to watch the Red Wings take on the Phoenix Coyotes at 6:00 p.m.

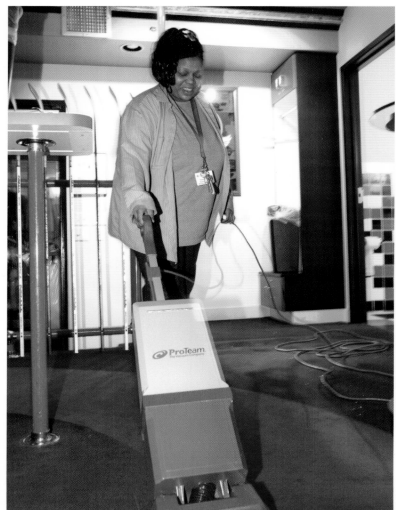

(above) Tonight's game will air both locally on UPN-50 and nationally on ESPN as part of ESPN's Sunday Night Hockey telecasts.

(right) With over 78 executive suites and five super suites inside Joe Louis Arena, the task of keeping each one neat and tidy is a full-time job during the 41-game regular season.

(below) Food preparation must begin early in order to accommodate the hundreds of guests who will dine inside Joe Louis Arena's Olympia Club prior to tonight's game.

(left) Where's the beef? On game days, it can be found on the open fire in each of Joe Louis Arena's full-size kitchens, in preparation for that night's Olympia Club and executive-suite guests.

(above) Hot dogs and sporting events have always gone hand in hand - so much so that 40 racks of Brown's hot dog buns are delivered fresh on the morning of each Red Wings' game. Each rack contains 10 dozen hot dog buns.

(above left) Red Wings' assistant athletic trainer Russ Baumann and Senior Director of Communications John Hahn keep a close eye on Jiri Fischer as he continues to recover from a torn anterior cruciate ligament suffered only 15 games into the 2002-03 season.

(above right) Fischer has been skating on his own for over two weeks now and is hopeful to get back in the Wings' lineup before season's end.

(opposite below) Fischer would return to practice with the team only a few weeks later, but ultimately would not dress for a game during the remainder of the year.

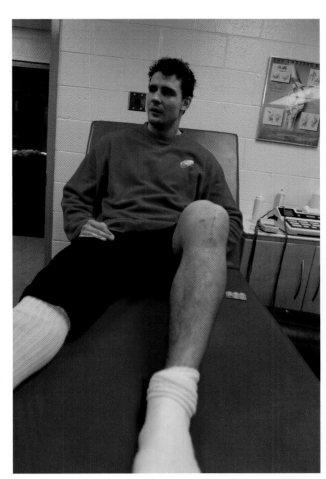

(opposite) Coyotes' Manager of Broadcasting Graham Taylor (above) and Producer for Fox Sports Net Arizona Jim Armintrout (below) sit in the stands and discuss tonight's contest as the Coyotes take the ice for their morning skate.

(left) After missing the majority of the season with a groin injury, Coyotes' goaltender Sean Burke is back in the lineup and will start in tonight's game.

(above) Arriving early to watch the players take the ice for their morning skate, this young fan eagerly awaits this evening's contest.

(above) Imposing steel doors adorned with one of sport's most recognized emblems - the winged wheel - stand at the main entrance to the Wings' newly constructed dressing room.

(left) Just behind the steel doors lies the hallway leading into the Wings' dressing room. To the right, the Wings' main stick rack houses each player's favorite piece of lumber. To the left, plaques display the Red Wings who are enshrined in the Hockey Hall of Fame.

(above) A closer look at the door leading directly into the dressing room reveals specially constructed winged-wheel doorknobs.

(above left) Assistant equipment-manager Tim Abbot straightens all of the locker stalls in preparation for tonight's game.

(above right) A staple in all hockey dressing rooms, multi-colored tape sits neatly stacked.

(right) The Red Wings' dressing room received a complete make-over during the summer of 2002. A finished look at the room showcases the players' stalls, complete with equipment, benches and storage units.

(above left) A glove sits on the glove dryer inside the locker room. The dryer blows warm air through the tubes to speed up the drying process, and holds up to seven pairs of gloves at once.

(below left) This stack of free weights sits in the Wings' exercise area, which also includes stationary bikes and a variety of other exercise equipment.

(above and right) Inside the players' lounge, several jerseys sit on the granite buffet counter, waiting for autographs. The new lounge was expanded from 100 square feet to over 700 square feet during the Red Wings' locker-room renovation during the summer of 2002.

(above) Curtis Joseph's infamous "Cujo" mask - one of the most recognizable masks in the NHL today - sits on the top of his stall.

(left) Inside the Red Wings' new state-of-the-art video room, associate coach Barry Smith reviews highlights from the Wings' game against the Toronto Maple Leafs. Smith and the Red Wings would usually be on the ice at this time, but the coaching staff has given the team the morning off in light of tonight's early 6:00 p.m. face off.

(above and above right) Coyotes' equipment manager Stan Wilson sharpens skates in the hallway leading to the visitors' locker room. As is the case with all NHL equipment managers, he brings his own skate sharpener on the road.

(right) After Phoenix leaves the ice, a guest of Coyotes' scout Warren Reichel, gets a chance to shoot a few pucks on the Joe Louis Arena ice.

(right) Ladislav Nagy (left) and Radislav Suchy (right) head out to the team bus en route to the Atheneum Suites in downtown Detroit. There they will gather for the pre-game meal prior to game time.

(above right) An old street sign from I-75 hangs on the concourse wall as a reminder of Olympia Stadium, the Red Wings' stomping grounds for 52 years.

(below right) Coyotes' captain Teppo Numminen stops to sign a few autographs on his way to the bus. Numminen is the center of numerous trade rumors that project him landing in Detroit before the trade deadline. These rumors would prove to be false as the Red Wings will acquire Mathieu Schneider from Los Angeles on March 11th.

(left) A shot, taken through a hole in the glass that referees use when communicating with off-ice officials, shows Mark Gier from the Red Wings' operations staff working on the official scorer's table.

(above right) A technician for ESPN tapes one of 12 microphones around the arena that will be used to heighten the audio along the boards during ESPN's telecast of tonight's game.

(below right) Raymond Cendrowski finishes up his duties of waxing the inside and outside of each pane of glass around the rink. This task is completed before every Red Wings' home game.

Joe Louis Arena's Sony® Video Wall is one of only two in existence - the Hartford Civic Center houses the other. The structure weighs over 10 tons and is seen here being repaired before tonight's contest.

(opposite) Inside the arena's carpentry room, Dave Gurdziel cuts new pieces of glass to be used on top of the boards. There are always at least 10 pre-cut pieces of glass on hand during every home game in case any are shattered during the action.

(above right) Up on the main concourse, vendors begin to stock their shelves with Red Wings merchandise, including one of the 15 different types of available bobbleheads.

(below right) Nelson Pageau (left) and George Gondec (right) have been vendors at Joe Louis Arena since the mid-'70s. In all, the two have over 100 years of vending experience in the Detroit area, having also worked for the Lions and Tigers.

(opposite) Opened in 1979, the Olympia Club - located in the Joe Louis Arena's west end - has entertained thousands of its members during Red Wings' home games.

(above right) Inside the Olympia Club, 130 tables are set for tonight's guests. Members of the club can enjoy fine dining and cocktails prior to, during, and after every home game.

(below right) The original décor of the club features old wood from Olympia Stadium, while the walls are adorned with framed photos of Red Wing greats.

(left) One of hockey's trademark symbols - the Zamboni® ice resurfacer - sits in its parking spot prior to tonight's game. This giant machine weighs over 13,000 pounds when filled with water.

(above) Inside Joe Louis Arena's "keg room," Maurice Majors checks the line running into one of the hundreds of beer kegs in the room. In all, over 21,000 feet of beer lines run from this room to the various concession stands around the arena.

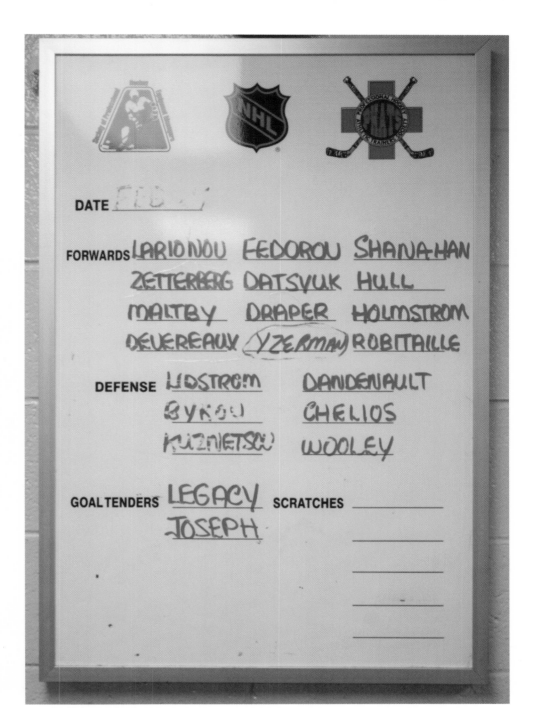

DATE _____

FORWARDS LARIONOU FEDOROU SHANAHAN
ZETTERBERG DATSYUK HULL
MALTBY DRAPER HOLMSTROM
DEVEREAUX (YZERMAN) ROBITAILLE

DEFENSE LIDSTROM DANDENAULT
BYKOV CHELIOS
KUZNETSOU WOOLEY

GOALTENDERS LEGACY SCRATCHES _____
JOSEPH _____
_____
_____
_____
_____

(above left) The Coyotes' locker room is ready for game time, as all the players' equipment and jerseys are laid out in anticipation of their arrival.

(above right) A dry-erase board in the visitors' locker room shows the writing from the Red Wings' game on February 24th against Los Angeles. Steve Yzerman's name is circled to signify his return to the Wings' lineup after off-season knee surgery, while someone has misspelled the names of goaltender Manny Legace and defenseman Jason Woolley.

(below left) The jersey of then-Phoenix forward Tony Amonte hangs in the corner of the locker room. Only eight days later, Amonte will be dealt to the Philadelphia Flyers on trade-deadline day.

(right) Frank Alvarado mops the lower concourse floor prior to the arrival of both teams as well as the media later in the day.

(opposite above) Registration for a Detroit Red Wings/Coca-Cola® Kids' Camp begins as approximately 100 kids will get the opportunity to take to the ice with former-Red Wing Mickey Redmond at 4 p.m.

(opposite below) One of the Kids' Camp participants laces up his skates before taking the ice.

Red Wings' athletic trainer Piet Van Zant takes care of some paperwork before the players arrive for treatment a few hours prior to the game.

CHAPTER TWO

Warming Up the Ice

(previous page) Kris Draper, who is always the first player on the ice, leads the Red Wings out of the locker room for tonight's pre-game skate.

(opposite left) Ken Kal sits down to interview head-coach Dave Lewis inside the coaches' room. Kal will use the material for tonight's pre-game show on AM 1270 The Sports Station.

(opposite right) After finishing a pre-game workout, assistant-coach Joe Kocur reviews tonight's game notes that include rosters, stats and player bios for both the Red Wings and Coyotes.

(above) Former 50-goal scorer and current Red Wings' television analyst Mickey Redmond gives instructions to a few lucky youngsters at center ice.

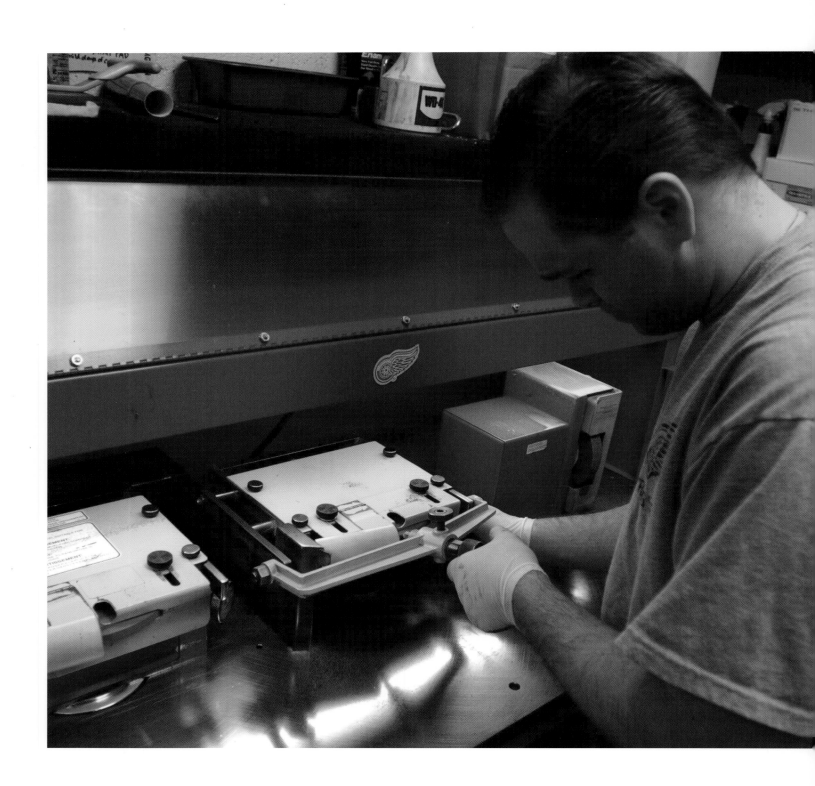

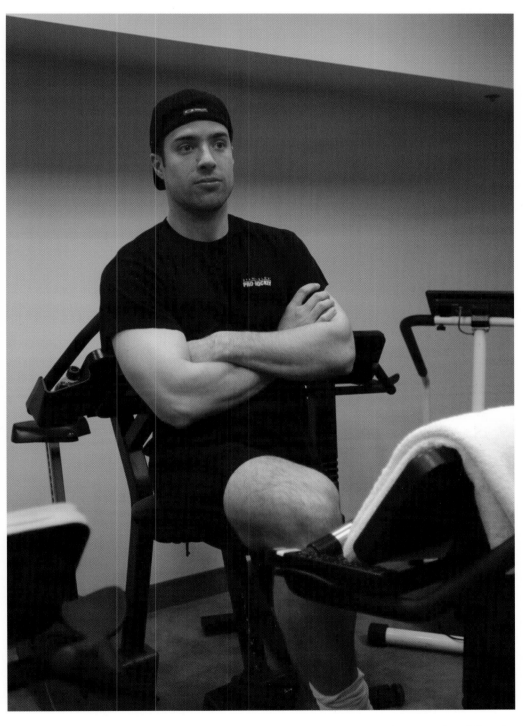

(opposite) While the kids are on the ice, preparation for tonight's game is already well underway in the Wings' locker room as equipment-manager Paul Boyer dresses the sharpening wheel on his skate sharpener.

(above) Since the Red Wings did not have a morning skate, defenseman Patrick Boileau loosens up by riding one of the more than 20 stationary bikes inside the Wings' weight room.

Red Wings' Senior Director of Communications John Hahn sits and chats with Brett Hull inside the Red Wings' all-new 7,830-square-foot locker room.

(left) Defenseman Maxim Kuznetsov unwinds in the locker room by doing a crossword puzzle. Kuznetsov will be a healthy scratch for tonight's contest, and will be traded in a few weeks to Los Angeles.

(right) Video-coordinator Mike Kruzelynski titles a tape of highlights from the Red Wings' last game against Phoenix.

(above) Goaltender Curtis Joseph (left) and rookie Henrik Zetterberg (right) get treatment prior to the game from Red Wings' athletic trainers Piet Van Zant (left) and Russ Bauman (right).

(left) Dmitri Bykov and Pavel Datsyuk prepare their sticks for tonight's contest. Both Bykov and Datsyuk prefer the one-piece Easton model.

(above) Players have their own personal preferences when it comes to taping their sticks. Color, thickness, and even superstition, all play a role in how the sticks are taped.

(above) Mathieu Dandenault (right) and Jason Woolley (left) prepare their sticks for tonight's game in the locker room. The wood used throughout the room is maple-stained cherry to compliment the red and white uniforms.

(left) Each stick is lined up according to the player's sweater number, meaning that Tomas Holmstrom - who wears #96 - can find his at the end of the rack.

(above) Deciding that he needs one more stick, Tomas Holmstrom saws off the end of the stick to make it shorter.

(below left) Kirk Maltby watches in the background as rookie Henrik Zetterberg measures the length of his new Easton Synergy stick.

(below right) Maltby shortens his stick by choosing to use a different saw than Tomas Holmstrom.

(above) Nicklas Lidstrom ties up his shoes before his stretching routine. The warm-up skate is a short time away and the players will begin to get dressed in uniform.

The Phoenix Coyotes arrive at
Joe Louis Arena around two
hours prior to game time.

(above) While the players prepare in the locker rooms, the press begins to gather in the media room for the pre-game meal. Long-time Red Wings' colleague Leslie Robart serves up tonight's pre-game meal to UPN-50's sport's anchor Ray Lane.

(below) NHL off-ice officials Jack Hughes (left) and George Blanchard (right) enjoy their own pre-game meal before going to work.

(above right) Red Wings' General Manager Ken Holland (right) discusses trade-deadline options with Coyotes' Senior VP of Hockey Operations Cliff Fletcher.

(above) Coyotes' General Manager Michael Barnett joins in the conversation with Fletcher and Holland.

(right) With the Kids' Camp all over, Mickey Redmond takes off his skates in an auxiliary locker room near the Joe Louis Arena ice. Redmond is happy to be back on skates after recovering from major surgery three months earlier to remove cancerous tissue from his lungs.

(opposite) Red Wings' assistant masseur Daryl Pittman stretches out Kirk Maltby prior to the pre-game skate.

(above) ESPN announcers Dave Strader (left) and Darren Pang (right) share a laugh with Ken Holland outside of the Red Wings' locker room. The Red Wings' equipment truck sits in the background awaiting the trip to Metro Airport immediately after the game.

(opposite above) Barnko Radivojevic (left) and Brad May (right) work on their sticks in the hallway of the visitors' locker room.

(opposite below) Ken Holland discusses some minor Red Wings' injuries with team physician Dr. David Collon, who has been with the Red Wings for the past 14 seasons.

Last-minute equipment checks are made before the Red Wings take to the ice for the pre-game skate. One of the superstitions of the Red Wings is to never step on the winged-wheel logo in the middle of the locker room floor.

(opposite) Darren McCarty (left), Daryl Pittman (middle) and Patrick Boileau (right) catch the last round of the WGC-Accenture Match Play tournament in the Red Wings' new custom-designed players' lounge that includes cherry wood private lockers, a granite buffet table and a big-screen TV.

(left) Art Regner hosts his Red Wings pre-game show on AM 1270 The Sports Station from inside studio "P," a converted bathroom just outside the Red Wings' locker room.

(above) Brett Hull quickly became one of the Red Wings' most consistent goal-scorers since his arrival in 2001. He would sign a contract extension with the Red Wings just three weeks after the game, to secure his roster spot for the 2003-04 season.

(below) Mathieu Dandenault tries multiple sticks during the warm-ups. Dandenault is one of many Red Wings who use the new Easton Synergy one-piece composite stick instead of the traditional two-piece model.

(opposite) Brendan Shanahan works on his puck-handling during the pre-game skate. He would go on to record 30 goals for the sixth time in his seven seasons with the Red Wings.

(right) Fellow members of Team USA, Chris Chelios and Tony Amonte chat during pre-game warm-ups. Amonte and Chelios played together in the 1998 and 2002 Winter Olympics, as well as during their four years together with the Chicago Blackhawks.

(opposite) Sergei Fedorov takes a shot on goaltender Manny Legace. Legace will back up starting-goaltender Curtis Joseph in tonight's contest.

(opposite) Curtis Joseph attempts to juggle the floating puck with his goal stick.

(above) The Red Wings use two different kinds of pucks on game days. Their pre-game pucks are sponsored by Powerade® and include the Red Wings logo on one side. Actual game pucks are licensed by the National Hockey League and are kept frozen until game time to ensure a smoother slide on the ice.

(above left) Darren McCarty looks around for extra pucks that he will use for his pre-game routine of throwing them into the stands for the kids in the crowd.

(above right) Kirk Maltby walks off the ice and back into the Red Wings' locker room. The players will have an extra five or six minutes to prepare while the ice is re-surfaced.

(opposite) Maxim Kuznetsov, one of the tallest players ever to don a Red Wings jersey, heads back to the locker room. He will be a healthy scratch tonight to make room for Jesse Wallin in the lineup.

(opposite) The Red Wings' coaching staff puts the finishing touches on tonight's lineup card that will be signed and turned over to the NHL's off-ice officials. Tonight's scratches include Patrick Boileau, Maxim Kuznetsov and Steve Yzerman.

(above) Paul Boyer makes one last pass by the stick rack to make sure the players have everything they need before the game starts.

Barry Smith makes his pass through the dressing room, reminding the defensemen of their assignments. Tonight's task is for Nicklas Lidstrom and Mathieu Dandenault to contain the Coyotes' scoring threat of Tony Amonte and Daniel Briere.

(above) Luc Robitaille, the highest-scoring left wing in NHL history, takes a moment for final pre-game preparation. This will be Robitaille's last season in Detroit as he will become a free agent over the summer.

(opposite) Tomas Holmstrom mentally prepares for the physical challenge that lies ahead.

With only a few minutes before the pucks drops, Brendan Shanahan follows behind Sergei Fedorov onto the ice. Shanahan, a left wing, always waits in the hallway until his center for that night exits the locker room. He then jumps in line behind his center and follows him onto the ice.

CHAPTER THREE
Detroit Red Wings vs. Phoenix Coyotes

CHAPTER THREE
Detroit Red Wings vs. Phoenix Coyotes

(*previous page*) Brendan Shanahan, Luc Robitaille,
Sergei Fedorov, and Mathieu Dandenault celebrate
Nicklas Lidstrom's (not shown) third-period goal
that put the Red Wings up 5-1 over Phoenix.

(opposite) Karen Newman warms up her vocal chords just prior to singing the national anthem.

(above) A staple at Joe Louis Arena, Karen Newman has been singing the national anthem at Red Wings' games for over eight years and has become a fixture in Hockeytown.

(right) No other NHL arena in the United States can boast as many Stanley Cup banners as Joe Louis Arena. The Red Wings' tenth championship banner was hung from the rafters on October 17th, 2002. Only Montreal (24) and Toronto (13) have won the Cup more times.

(opposite) A Detroit police officer salutes the American flag during Karen Newman's rendition of the national anthem.

(above) A view from the Joe Louis Arena catwalk shows the starting lineups just prior to the opening face-off.

(opposite) Sergei Fedorov tries to avoid the hook given by Coyotes' defenseman Todd Simpson.

(previous page) Coyotes' goaltender Brian Boucher and defenseman Radoslav Suchy await a wrist shot from the stick of Pavel Datsyuk. The inset shot shows the same action, but from a different angle.

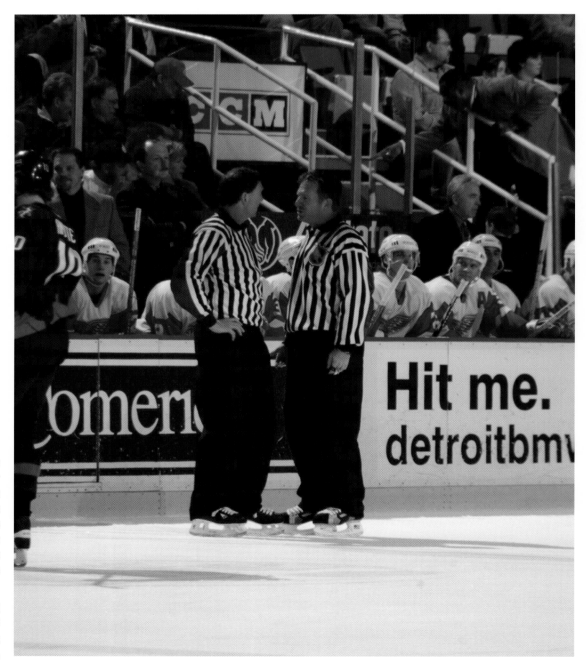

(above) Tomas Holmstrom tries to dig a loose puck out of the corner during a physical first period. From this angle, it's easy to notice the extra padding that Holmstrom tapes to the back of his legs. The extra padding protects him from the slashes he receives in front of the net.

(right) Referees Kevin Collins and Danny McCourt discuss the penalty for too many men on the ice, given to the Red Wings in the first period.

(above) A creative young fan displays her Red Wings passion with her Wing-nut hat, complete with octopus doll and pompoms.

(above) A look from above shows the Sony® Video Wall hanging above the ice. The structure's television walls house a total of 64 television screens on the four sides combined.

(opposite above left) Kris Draper hustles to get back in the play as the Red Wings kill off the Coyotes' second power play of the period.

(opposite above right) Brett Hull makes a turn to follow a loose puck in the Coyotes' end of the ice.

(opposite below) After chasing a loose puck, Darren McCarty pays the price by getting checked into the boards by Coyotes' forward Daymond Langkow.

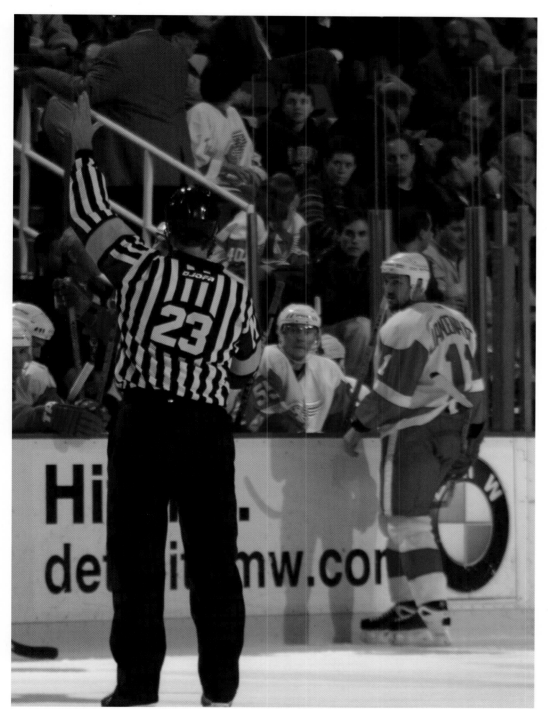

(opposite above) Offering a great view of the action, a night in one of Joe Louis Arena's 82 executive suites is often the hottest ticket in town.

(opposite below) A view from an executive level suite shows the action at ice level.

(left) Referee Brad Watson calls Sergei Fedorov for kneeing at 18:51 of a scoreless first period.

(right) UPN-50's Ray Lane takes time to interview Tomas Holmstrom during the first intermission. Holmstrom would go on to set a career-high record this season with 20 goals.

(below) A lucky fan gets to play the Score-O contest during the first intermission.

(opposite) Kaitlyn Rots gets a ride on the Miller Lite Zamboni® during the first intermission.

(right) Fans line up during the intermission at one of the seven merchandise stands open at Joe Louis Arena during the game.

(below) Merchandise stands sell everything you can think of - from jerseys and hats to car flags and bobbleheads.

(above) A thirsty fan waits for his libation during a break in the game's action. On average, Joe Louis Arena fans consume a total of around 1,600 gallons of beer per game.

(opposite) An ESPN cameraman shoots the teams returning to the ice for the beginning of the second period.

(above) On the fresh new ice surface, Nicklas Lidstrom controls the puck and plays "keep away" as the Red Wings' penalty-killing unit tries to stifle the Coyotes' power play.

(below) Chris Chelios watches in the background as rookie Dmitri Bykov moves the puck up the ice while the Wings are on the penalty-kill.

(above) The NHL off-ice officials keep a close eye on the action as they keep track of stats like hits, turnovers, face-offs and goals.

(above left) Ken Daniels and Mickey Redmond use their monitor to review a play during the second period.

(above right) Long-time public address announcer Budd Lynch has been with the Red Wings organization for over 50 years, beginning as a radio announcer with fellow-Hall of Famer Bruce Martyn.

(left) ESPN announcers Dave Strader (left) and Darren Pang (right) prepare to return from a television time-out.

(previous page) Curtis Joseph keeps the game scoreless as he makes one of his 14 second-period saves in spectacular fashion.

(opposite) Fans show their support for Curtis Joseph after he makes a save. Joseph signed on as a free agent in July of 2002.

(above) The production room on the top level of Joe Louis Arena controls the video and audio feeds throughout the entire arena, along with those at Hockeytown Cafe - a Red Wings-themed restaurant over a mile away.

(right) With the game still scoreless, Tomas Holmstrom, Kris Draper and Kirk Maltby make a push up the ice in an attempt to keep the pressure on the Coyotes' end.

(right) Fans celebrate Brett Hull's goal at 10:40 of the second period, giving the Red Wings a 1-0 lead. The goal is his 27th of the season.

(above) Coyotes' goaltender Brian Boucher looks down to try to find the puck before realizing that Brett Hull's slapshot sneaked through the five-hole, giving the Red Wings a 1-0 lead.

(below left) Chris Chelios chases Coyotes' forward Ladislav Nagy into the corner of the ice.

(below right) Just over a minute after Hull scored, Phoenix defenseman Teppo Numminen (not shown) beats Curtis Joseph over the left shoulder to tie the game at one.

(above) Athletic trainer Piet Van Zant helps Chris Chelios off the ice after he re-aggravates a knee injury from earlier in the year. Chelios would not return to the game, nor would he play in the following game against Columbus.

(opposite) With the second period winding down and the Red Wings up 3-1 after goals from Pavel Datsyuk and Henrik Zetterberg, Darren McCarty and Drake Berehowsky draw a crowd near center ice as they duke it out. McCarty would receive a 10-minute major for the altercation, while Berehowsky only received a five-minute fighting penalty.

(right) The iceman himself, Al Sobotka, resurfaces the ice during the second intermission. Sobotka has been the Red Wings' iceman since the early '70s.

(above) Fans line up to buy Little Caesars pizza during the second intermission. On average, the pizza stands will go through 1,300 pounds of dough, 700 pounds of cheese, 45 gallons of sauce and 41,000 pepperonis during one Red Wings' home game.

(left) Dominique Horton molds dough into a pan as vendors try to keep up with the high demand during the intermissions.

(opposite) Replicas of the Red Wings' 10 Stanley Cup banners hang in the concourse of Joe Louis Arena.

(above) The Sony® Video Wall shows only two minutes remaining in the second intermission. Phoenix will start the third period with 19 seconds remaining on their power play after Kirk Maltby was called for unsportsmanlike conduct at 18:19 of the second period.

(above) Curtis Joseph and Kris Draper lead the Red Wings back on the ice for the third period with a two-goal lead, 3-1.

(opposite above) Amongst a hoard of players, Curtis Joseph makes one of his 22 saves of the night.

(above) While their dads work on the ice, Max Holmstrom (left) and Sam Lidstrom (right) play on Joe Louis Arena's lower concourse just outside of the Red Wings' family room.

(above) Scott Pellerin and Radoslav Sucy look on as Pavel Datsyuk's second goal of the game slips past Brian Boucher at 5:37 of the third period. The goal was Datsyuk's ninth of the season, giving the Red Wings a commanding 4-1 lead.

(opposite) Jesse Wallin and Henrik Zetterberg congratulate Pavel Datsyuk on his third-period goal and his fourth point of the night. Datsyuk would go on to tally 11 points total for his next three games and tonight's game.

(above) Brendan Shanahan carries the puck up the left side next to Luc Robitaille. Shanahan would eventually pass to Sergei Fedorov, who would then set up Nicklas Lidstrom for the Red Wings' fifth goal of the game.

(opposite above) Luc Robitaille and Nicklas Lidstrom await the rest of their teammates as they celebrate Lidstrom's 13th goal of the season, giving the Red Wings a 5-1 lead.

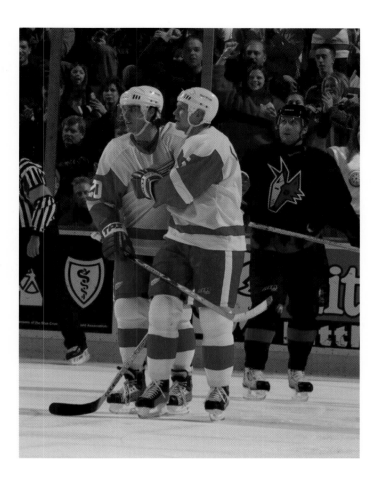

(left) The Phoenix Coyotes celebrate Drake Berehowsky's goal at 8:54 of the third period. Although it would narrow the score to 5-2, it's as close as Phoenix would get.

(opposite) The Red Wings bench looks on as they begin to sense their ninth win in the past 10 games.

(above) With tonight's game in hand, the Red Wings' coaching staff knows that the Wings have crept two points closer to the Western Conference-leading Dallas Stars.

(below) With only 18 games remaining on their schedule, tonight's loss will make it very difficult for the Coyotes to catch the Edmonton Oilers for the eighth and final playoff spot in the Western Conference.

(opposite) Pavel Datsyuk just misses his first career hat trick as he sends this wrist shot just wide of Brian Boucher and the Phoenix net.

(above) Just after Datsyuk missed the net, Darren McCarty rings a wrister off the post that would have given Detroit a 6-2 lead.

(opposite) A young fan reacts to Darren McCarty's shot that rang off the post as time winds down in the contest.

(above) After time expires, the Red Wings congratulate Curtis Joseph on his 31st victory of the year, moving the Red Wings within five points of the Western Conference-leading Dallas Stars.

(left) With a goal and an assist, rookie Henrik Zetterberg is named the game's third star. Zetterberg would go on to finish second in the Calder Trophy voting behind St. Louis' Barret Jackman for Rookie of the Year.

Pavel Datsyuk acknowledges the cheers of the Joe Louis Arena crowd after being named the game's first star with two goals and two assists.

CHAPTER FOUR
Leaving on a Jet Plane

(previous page) Sergei Fedorov arrives at Signature Air in Romulus, Michigan, before he and the rest of the Red Wings board Red Bird II en route to Columbus.

(*opposite*) Curtis Joseph and Tomas Holmstrom hurry to shed their equipment and get it into their equipment bags.

(*above*) The players' equipment bags will eventually be stacked on the cart in the middle of the locker room. Their bags will then be loaded onto the equipment truck before heading out to the airport.

(right) After the game, the Zamboni® machine resurfaces the ice. It has a large bin in front to collect ice shavings scraped by a blade in the conditioner, behind the rear tires. Tanks underneath the bin and in front of the driver store water for conditioning and cleaning the ice.

(above) Henrik Zetterberg takes time to speak with the media about his performance and the strong play of his line-mates Brett Hull and Pavel Datsyuk.

(left) Once out of his uniform, Kris Draper visits with his wife Julie and daughter Kennedi just outside of the Red Wings' locker room.

(previous page) Not long after the final whistle has blown, the Red Wings' locker stalls are completely emptied and packed away for tonight's trip to Columbus.

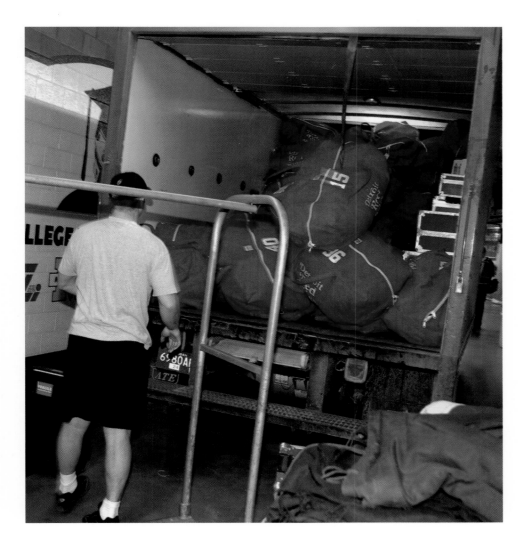

(opposite) On nights when the Red Wings travel, the standard is to be "wheels-up in four hours," meaning they take off in Red Bird II four hours after the opening face off. With games sometimes lasting three hours, preparing for post-game travel is often hectic.

(left) The Red Wings' equipment truck not only hauls the Wings' equipment back and forth from the airport, but also assists visiting teams when they come to town.

(below) Mathieu Dandenault treats the same group of excited fans to autographs on his way out.

(above left) Fellow Swedes Tomas Holmstrom and Nicklas Lidstrom leave Joe Louis Arena with their families.

(above right) Head-coach Dave Lewis walks alongside building manager Al Sobotka on his way out of the arena.

(opposite) Kris Draper says goodbye to his daughter Kennedi before he leaves for the airport. This will be a quick road trip for the Red Wings as they play Columbus and return home from Ohio tomorrow night.

(opposite) The crew at Signature Air in Romulus, Michigan, awaits the arrival of the Red Wings. The Wings' private jet - Red Bird II - sits just outside of the building, gassed up and ready to go.

(above) Curtis Joseph walks through the terminal on his way to the plane. Players are responsible for their own luggage on road trips. Since the Wings will only be gone for one night, most players have just one carry-on bag to worry about on this trip.

(right) Once aboard the plane, players mingle and have a bite to eat prior to take off. Tonight's flight will be delayed for almost 25 minutes while the Wings wait for Chris Chelios to return from having his injured knee looked at by doctors.

(below) Red Bird II has the capability of serving catered food, as the plane is equipped with warmers so players and staff can always have a warm meal.

(above) Red Bird II is divided into three sections: a spot up front for coaches to review video, a middle section dubbed "the quiet zone" for rest and relaxation, and a back section, as shown here, with groups of chairs and tables used for recreation.

(above) Once in the air, Red Wings Media Relations Manager Mike Kuta works on the night's game notes in preparation for tomorrow's game against Columbus. Kuta is responsible for supplying all members of the media with the most up-to-date information on the team.

(above and below) After the short 35-minute flight to Columbus, Darren McCarty (above), Igor Larionov (below) and the rest of the Red Wings exit the plane and board their awaiting charter bus en route to the team's hotel.

(right) As the players board the bus for the hotel, Columbus Blue Jackets equipment assistant Andre Szucko waits to load up the Red Wings equipment before heading to Nationwide Arena.

(middle) A conveyor belt guides the Red Wings equipment from the plane and into the awaiting truck. Red Wings athletic trainers Piet Van Zant and Russ Baumann, along with equipment manager Paul Boyer and team masseur Sergei Tchekmarev will make the trip to the Nationwide Arena to set up the Red Wings locker room for tomorrow's morning skate.

(below) Once inside Nationwide Arena, Blue Jackets equipment assistant Andre Szucko helps Red Wings athletic trainer Piet Van Zant unload the truck.

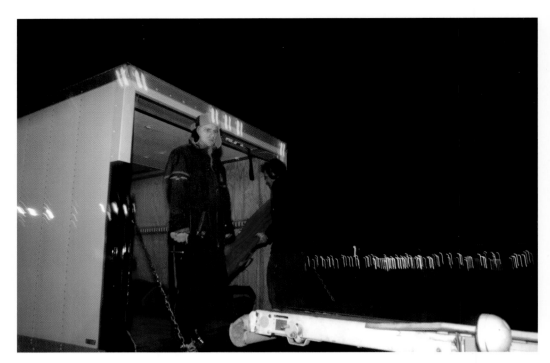

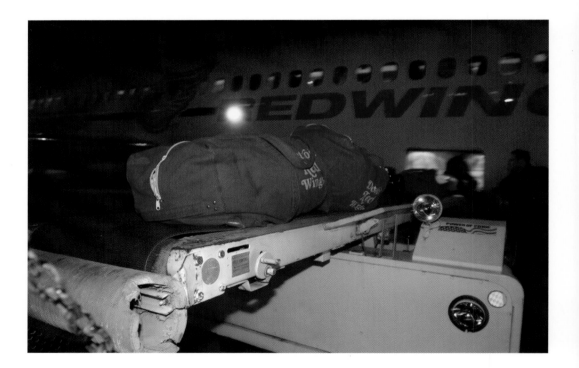

(above) Although it's approaching midnight, the evening is still early for the Red Wings staff, including athletic trainer Piet Van Zant. They must still set up the Wings locker room for the morning skate now less than 10 hours away.

(previous page) A time-lapse sequence shows the Red Wings visiting dressing room transformed from an empty space to a fully stocked room. The project would take the Red Wings staff well over an hour to complete as their day finally ends at around 1:30 a.m.

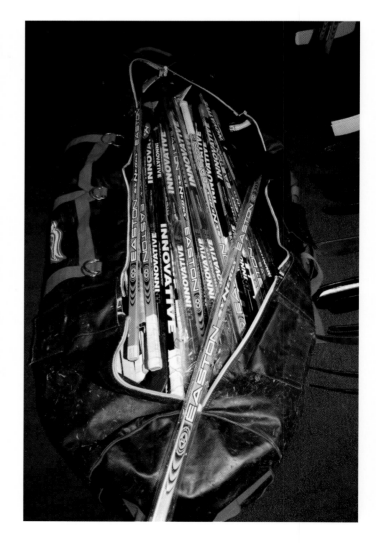

(opposite above) Piet Van Zant unloads the Red Wings stick bag next to the glove dryers in the locker room. The dryers, along with a host of other equipment, are provided to the visiting teams by the home teams throughout the NHL.

(opposite below left) Andre Szucko pushes a cart full of Red Wings equipment down the hall and into the Red Wings locker room.

(opposite below right) With this being only a one-game road trip the players have brought along only a few sticks apiece. On longer trips, equipment manager Paul Boyer will be sure to bring along plenty more.

(left) An industrial size fan dries out Curtis Joseph's goaltender pads. The fan will run all through the night to make sure everything is dry by the morning.

In order to dry out every player's skates, Boyer lines them up in stacked semi-circle so that the fan can blow directly into them and dry them out in time for the morning skate.

CHAPTER FIVE

Rise and Shine on the Road

(previous page)
Darren McCarty walks two blocks from the Red Wings' hotel to Nationwide Arena for the Wings' morning skate.

(above) In the heart of downtown Columbus, the NHL's newest hockey city, the Columbus Convention Center sits across from the team hotel and kitty-corner from Nationwide Arena.

(left) Inside the team's hotel, Ken Kal chats with a few Red Wings' fans who have congregated in the lobby in hopes of seeing their favorite players leave for the morning skate.

(below) Red Wings General Manager Ken Holland sits with Paul Woods (left) and Ken Daniels (middle) for their morning coffee before heading to the arena.

(right) Having arrived in Columbus only nine hours earlier, Darren McCarty and Manny Legace grab a morning "pick-me-up" before they head to Nationwide Arena for the team's optional morning skate.

(below) A young fan and his father brave the March morning's frigid temperature, seeking a few autographs from the Red Wings.

(above) Nationwide Arena opened its doors in September of 2000. It is the only building in the NHL that has the team's practice facility attached to the arena where the team plays its games.

(opposite above and below) While the Red Wings are getting ready to take the ice, the Blue Jackets are finishing up their morning skate and their stretches inside the empty arena.

(above) The red practice jerseys line the stalls of the visiting locker room. Although this morning's skate is optional, the entire team will attend the skate.

(opposite) Curtis Joseph and Chris Chelios sit on the training table awaiting treatments. Chelios aggravated a knee injury the night before against Phoenix and is questionable for tonight's contest.

(left) Coaches Joe Kocur and Dave Lewis loosen their legs before the morning skate.

(*opposite above*) Darren McCarty works on a new stick after he broke one during last night's game against Phoenix.

(*opposite below*) All tools and hardware, including these nuts and bolts, are provided to the visiting teams in accordance with NHL regulations.

(*above*) The Red Wings' coaching staff catches up with Blue Jackets' assistant coach Gerard Gallant. Gallant played for 12 years in Detroit, including four consecutive seasons with 70-plus points each, from 1986-90.

Throwing on his shoulder pads, Steve Yzerman prepares for the morning skate. Tonight will be only his third game back in the lineup after returning from major off-season knee surgery that kept him on the bench for the season's first 61 games.

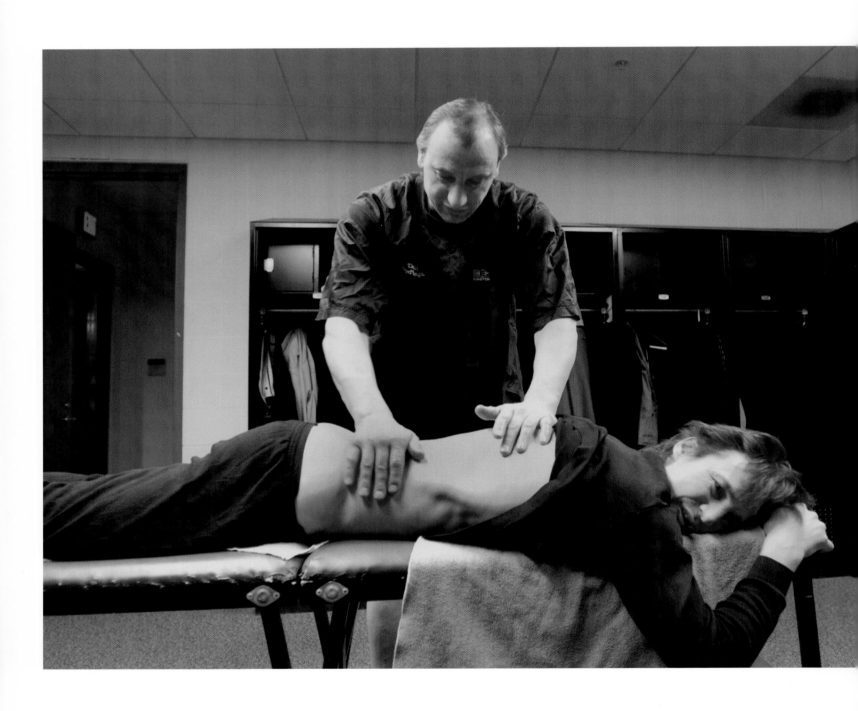

(opposite) Back in the Red Wings' dressing room, team masseur Sergei Tchekmarev tries to loosen up Sergei Fedorov's sore back.

(above) Manny Legace straps on his pads after learning that he will start in tonight's game in Columbus. Despite limited playing time all season, he has still managed to post a 10-4-3 record.

(right) It has been three days since Steve Yzerman has been on the ice. The Wings' coaching staff has been careful not to put too much stress on his knee.

(above) Joe Kocur (left) and Henrik Zetterberg (right) make their way onto the ice for the morning skate. Zetterberg would lead all NHL rookies in scoring during the season with 44 points.

(right) Darren McCarty walks onto the ice to loosen up. He earned a 10-minute major penalty in a fight last night against Phoenix.

(opposite) Steve Yzerman takes a shot on Manny Legace during the morning skate. Morning skates are held in order to stretch out the legs and go over last-minute strategies for the evening's contest.

(opposite) Claimed off waivers from Buffalo in November, Jason Woolley helped compensate for the loss of Jiri Fischer, who suffered a knee injury that would keep him out for the season. Woolley has proven to be a nice addition to the Wings' defensive corps with his strong skating and puck-moving skills.

(above) A lucky Red Wings' fan shows off his Wing-nut hat as he watches the morning skate.

(right) Steve Yzerman's return to the lineup has sent a feeling of relief throughout Hockeytown. After undergoing major reconstructive knee surgery during the off-season, skeptics believed that Yzerman's career might be over.

(opposite) Paul Boyer sharpens the skates of Curtis Joseph, who will be backing up Manny Legace in goal tonight.

(opposite) While the Wings are on the ice, Sergei Fedorov sits on the training table awaiting more treatment for his sore back. Fedorov will decide not to play in this evening's game, making it only the second game of the season without Fedorov in the lineup.

(above) With the morning skate almost over, head-coach Dave Lewis has come off the ice in favor of a spot on the bench.

(opposite) Ken Kal sits on the bench and reviews the night's game notes, preparing for his pre-game show and broadcast of tonight's game.

(above left) A Columbus reporter interviews Steve Yzerman after the morning skate. The NHL requires teams to open their locker rooms 10 minutes after morning skates and 10 minutes after games for media availability.

(above right) Detroit-area reporters Ted Kulfan (left) and Ansar Kahn (right) ask Chris Chelios about the status of his knee injury. Chelios tells them that he would not be in the lineup tonight for precautionary reasons.

(opposite) Jesse Wallin removes his pads after the morning skate. On average, when a player suits up with all of the NHL's required equipment, it can add as much as an extra 25 pounds to their body weight.

(above) Steve Yzerman continues to stretch out his knee on the stationary bike after the morning skate.

(above) In his morning briefing, Lewis once again tells reporters that Chris Chelios and Sergei Fedorov will not be in the lineup and that Steve Yzerman will play.

(opposite) On his way back to the hotel, Boyd Devereaux signs a puck for a fan.

Jason Woolley and Boyd Devereaux leave the arena in time to get back to the hotel for their pre-game meal and nap before having to return to the arena later in the afternoon.

CHAPTER SIX
Warming Up the Ice, Part II

(previous page) Brett Hull, a five-time 50-goal scorer, became the newest member of the NHL's exclusive 700-goal club on February 10th, 2003, against San Jose.

(above) The Red Wings have fans all around North America, but especially in Columbus. Inside the team hotel, hundreds of fans line up for a chance to see their favorite players, including this lucky fan who gets an autograph from Ken Kal.

(above left) The Red Wings' charter bus waits to take the team to Nationwide Arena. All of the team's luggage will be placed under the bus since they will not be returning to their rooms.

(above right) After a very short bus ride, the Red Wings arrive at Nationwide Arena two hours prior to the drop of the puck.

(left) Unable to bear the frigid temperatures anymore, a young Red Wings fan finds warmth inside his parent's van as they wait to see the Red Wings arrive at the arena.

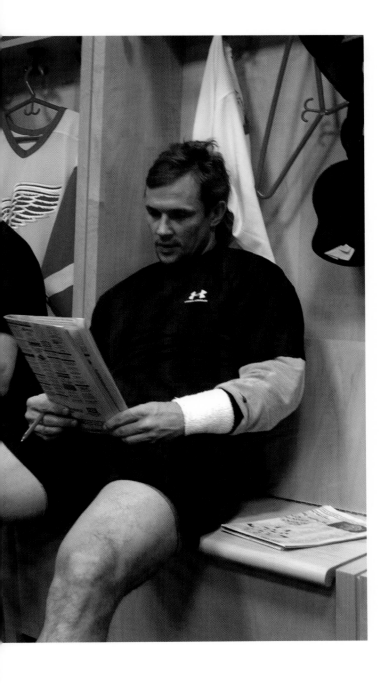

(opposite) Brendan Shanahan is one of the few Red Wings still using the traditional two-piece stick. He melts the glue on his stick with a blowtorch before sliding the blade over the stick and allowing it to dry.

(middle) With time to kill before throwing on his equipment, Steve Yzerman works on one of his favorite pre-game rituals: a crossword puzzle.

(above) Kris Draper goes through his routine pre-game stretch, doing drills up and down the empty hallway until his legs are loose.

(opposite) A look inside an empty Nationwide Arena shows the 18,136-seat venue that opened its doors in September of 2000.

(above) A view of center ice displays the Blue Jackets logo, which represents the Columbus area's participation in the Civil War. The 13 stars in the logo represent the original 13 colonies and patriotism.

(above) Stinger, the Blue Jackets' mascot, gives a hug to one of the members of the Pepsi® Power Patrol, who go around the arena during the game to pump up the crowd.

(above left and right) A large number of Red Wings fans make the trip to Columbus for these games due to its close proximity to the Detroit area. As a treat tonight, they will get to see Steve Yzerman play in his first road game of the season.

(opposite) Steve Yzerman stretches out his knee during the pre-game skate. Although the Red Wings usually wear their red jerseys on the road, they are in their whites tonight due to an earlier request from the Blue Jackets.

(left) Patrick Boileau stops to take a drink during the pre-game warm-up. He will, however, not be on the ice for tonight's game, as the coaching staff will decide to make him a healthy scratch in favor of Maxim Kuznetsov.

(above) Although he will not be starting tonight, Curtis Joseph still goes through his pre-game stretching, in case he is called upon to relieve Manny Legace.

(opposite) Tomas Holmstrom walks off the ice after the pre-game skate. A win tonight by the Red Wings will move them within three points of the Western Conference-leading Dallas Stars.

A look inside the locker room shows the Red Wings taking a breather only 15 minutes prior to the game. Notice how the players have their pads still on with the exception of Patrick Boileau (right side in black). Since he will be a healthy scratch tonight, he has taken off all of his equipment.

Manny Legace sits quietly as he begins to mentally prepare for the game. He will be looking for his third win in four career games against Columbus.

CHAPTER SEVEN

Detroit Red Wings vs. Columbus Blue Jackets

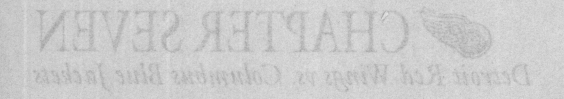

(previous page) In only his third game of the season, and first on the road, Steve Yzerman glances up at the scoreboard during the third period of the Red Wings' contest against Columbus.

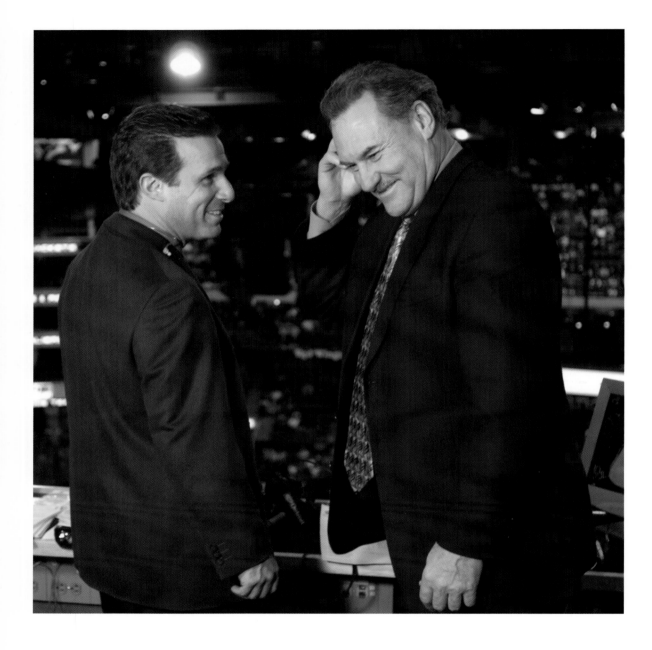

(opposite) Television announcers Ken Daniels (left) and Mickey Redmond (right) share a laugh during UPN-50's final commercial break before the puck drops between the Red Wings and Blue Jackets.

(above) Kris Draper wins the game's opening face-off against Blue Jackets' center Mike Sillinger. This is the fourth meeting between the two teams this season, with the Red Wings winning two and tying one.

(above) The Blue Jackets supply all of the offense power in the first period, out-shooting the Red Wings by 13-2 and forcing Manny Legace to make several big stops.

(left) Despite only two shots in the first period, the Red Wings found a way to get on the scoreboard, thanks to Brendan Shanahan's 24th goal of the season at 3:39 of the first. Pavel Datsyuk and Kris Draper picked up the assists.

(above) The Red Wings enjoy plenty of fan support every time they travel to Nationwide Arena. At times in the first period, the "Let's Go, Red Wings" chant could be heard.

(right) Who says you can't be friends with the opposition? These two girls sit and enjoy the game, displaying the jerseys of their favorite teams.

(right) If Manny Legace was rusty after playing only twice in the past two weeks, it certainly doesn't show during the first period as he makes one of his 13 saves in the period.

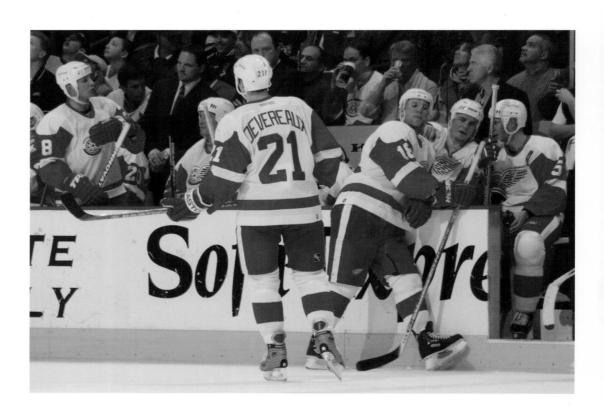

(above) During a television time-out, the Red Wings' penalty-killing unit gets some well-deserved rest. The Red Wings killed off four of five Columbus power plays during the first period alone.

(below) Nicklas Lidstrom attempts to break up a pass from Columbus' forward Geoff Sanderson. Only three months later, Lidstrom would go on to win his third consecutive Norris Trophy as the NHL's best defenseman.

(above) UPN-50's Ray Lane interviews Columbus forward Ray Whitney after the first period. Whitney's goal at 10:13 of the first tied the game at one.

(above) Just over two minutes into the second period, Brett Hull gives the Red Wings a 2-1 lead with his 29th goal of the season. Hull would go on to record 30 goals for the 12th time in his career, later in the week.

(right) Players huddle to celebrate Brett Hull's go-ahead goal. Jason Woolley and Pavel Datsyuk picked up the assists.

(above) Kris Draper nearly runs into Columbus goaltender Marc Denis during the second period. Denis would go on to play 4,511 minutes during the season - a new NHL single-season record.

(right) Kirk Maltby converses with Darren McCarty on the Red Wings bench during a Detroit power play in the second period.

(above) In only his third game back in the lineup, Steve Yzerman logged significant power-play time and won 11 of 16 face-offs.

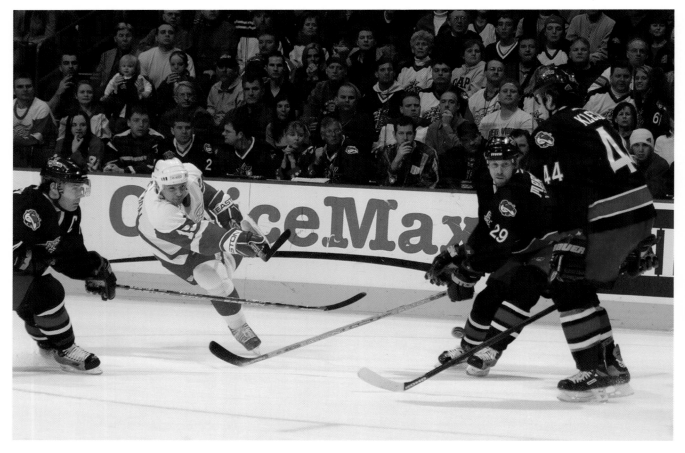

(above) The Red Wings cluster around the net as they look to go up by two goals.

(below) Defenseman Rastislav Klesla blocks Steve Yzerman's slapshot from the point. Klesla would tie the game at two with his first goal of the season at 10:19 of the second period.

(below) Columbus fans, along with Stinger the mascot, celebrate as they watch replays of Rastislav Klesla's goal on the overhead scoreboard.

(above left) A young hockey fan sits on his father's lap and tries to follow the action of his first hockey game.

(above right) Kirk Maltby gets restrained after being hit by Blue Jackets' forward Jean-Luc Grand-Pierre (not pictured). Grand-Pierre would receive a roughing penalty.

(above) On the ensuing Red Wings' power play, Igor Larionov carries the puck up the ice. At age 42, Larionov is the NHL's oldest player.

(right) Red Wings' forward Luc Robitaille tries to handle the puck before being checked into the boards by Blue Jackets' defenseman Jamie Allison.

(right) Red Wings Media Relations Manager Mike Kuta (in suit) pulls aside Jason Woolley for a second-intermission interview with UPN-50's Ray Lane.

(opposite) The 2002-03 hockey season was the last for Ray Lane and UPN-50. The long-time Red Wings' affiliate station concluded its broadcasts after 38 years of bringing Wings' games into the homes of hockey fans across the state.

(right) The Blue Jackets' Z a m b o n i ® does its best N A S C A R impersonation as it speeds by the camera while cleaning the ice for the third period.

(*left*) Fans are treated with highlights from the game's first two periods on the scoreboard as they wait for the third period.

(*below*) A pair of young friends sits together with their allegiances pledged to different sides.

(right) Brendan Shanahan eats an energy bar prior to the third period. He would go on to score the game-winner halfway through the period.

(below) Steve Yzerman wins the third period's opening face-off. He would win 11 of 16 face-offs during the night.

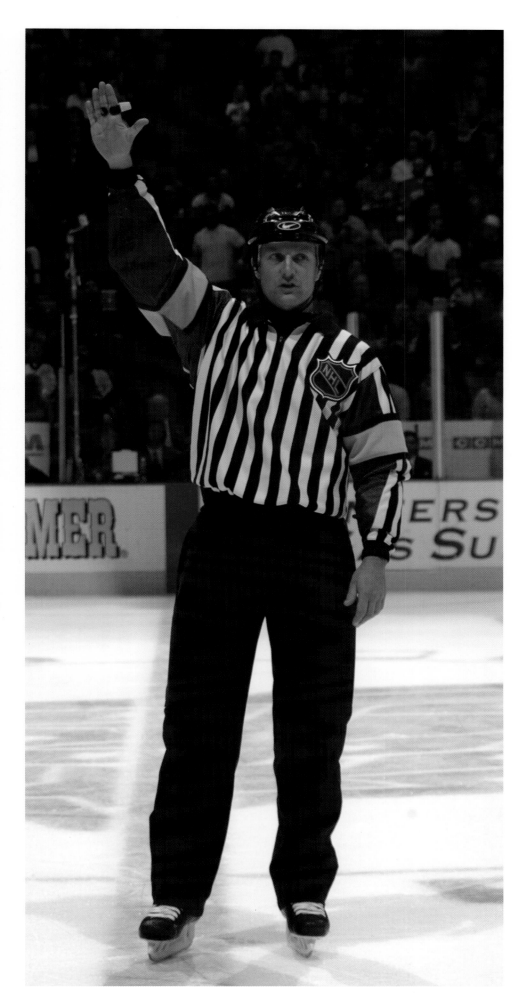

(left) Referee Brad Watson calls Blue Jackets' defenseman Jaroslav Spacek for boarding at 8:55 to put the Red Wings on the power play.

(opposite) Brendan Shanahan and teammates celebrate his game-winning goal at 9:39 of the third period. Pavel Datsyuk (not pictured) continued his hot play with his third assist on the goal and seventh point in the past two games.

(above) Trailing by one, the Columbus bench begins to feel the heat as time winds down in the contest.

(above) Today's gloves in the NHL are made up of about 90 individual pieces, including high or low-density foam to protect players' hands.

(above) Henrik Zetterberg and Tyler Wright battle for position for a loose puck in the third period.

(left) As time expires, Blue Jackets' rookie Rick Nash trips up Darren McCarty. Nash would finish the season third in both rookie scoring and Calder Trophy voting for the NHL's Rookie of the Year.

(above) Back in the visitors' locker room, the Red Wings relax as they enjoy their ninth victory in the past 10 games. The players will now pack their bags once again and head back to Detroit tonight.

(right) Manny Legace sits with a grin on his face after his 29-save performance, which resulted in a 3-2 Red Wings' victory and Legace's 11th win of the season.

(above left) Ray Lane interviews Brendan Shanahan who was named the game's first star with two goals, including the game-winner.

(above right) In the tunnel leading to the bench, a Columbus reporter interviews Jason Woolley after his two-assist performance.

(above) General Manager Ken Holland heads down the hallway on his way to the team's bus.

(right) Curtis Joseph boards the Red Wings' charter bus as it prepares to leave Nationwide Arena.

(above) On the bus, the Red Wings relax after winning consecutive games in just a little over a 24-hour span.

(above) The players board Red
Bird II for the short 35-minute
flight back to Detroit.

(above) An "up-close-and-personal" view into the cockpit shows the Red Wings' pilot preparing for take-off.

(left) Assistant coach Joe Kocur unwinds prior to take-off.

(opposite left) Kirk Maltby works on his laptop on the way home.

(opposite right) Athletic trainers Russ Baumann (left) and Piet Van Zant (right) look over the night's scorecard.

(above) Kris Draper offers a box of Paczkis to Ken Kal (not pictured) on the eve of Fat Tuesday, a Polish tradition held close to Kal's heart.

The Red Wings land back at
Detroit Metro Airport only
23 hours after they left. So
after two days, two flights,
two games and two
victories, their return to
Michigan marks the end of
the Wings' successful
48-hour journey.

Game Summary

2

PHOENIX COYOTES
Game 64 Away Game 33

Sunday, March 2, 2003
Attendance 20,058
at Joe Louis Arena
Start 6:09 PM ET;End 8:26 PM ET
Final

5

DETROIT RED WINGS
Game 64 Home Game 34

SCORING SUMMARY

G	Per	Time	Team	Goal Scorer	Assist	Assist	PHX	DET	STR
1	2	10:40	DET	B. HULL (27)	P. DATSYUK (19)	H. ZETTERBERG (15)	7 44 38 33 15 8	17 3 40 31 15 13	EV
2	2	11:48	PHX	T. NUMMINEN (3)	L. NAGY (27)	M. JOHNSON (34)	27 5 33 17 12 11	18 96 55 33 31 24	EV
3	2	13:03	DET	P. DATSYUK (8)	B. HULL (31)	J. WOOLLEY (17)	5 33 32 27 18 16	13 3 40 31 17 15	EV
4	2	17:43	DET	H. ZETTERBERG (15)	P. DATSYUK (20)	N. LIDSTROM (36)	7 33 27 12 11	40 5 91 31 17 13	PP
5	3	5:37	DET	P. DATSYUK (9)	B. HULL (32)		8 55 44 38 33 15	13 3 40 31 17 15	EV
6	3	6:58	DET	N. LIDSTROM (13)	S. FEDOROV (38)	B. SHANAHAN (28)	7 49 33 27 19 10	5 91 31 20 14 11	EV
7	3	8:54	PHX	D. BEREHOWSKY (1)	B. MAY (4)	K. BUCHBERGER (8)	5 55 33 32 18 16	13 55 40 31 25 15	EV

Game Summary

3

DETROIT RED WINGS
Game 65 Away Game 31

Monday, March 3, 2003
Attendance 18,136
at Nationwide Arena
Start 7:08 PM ET;End 9:25 PM ET
Final

2

COLUMBUS BLUE JACKETS
Game 65 Home Game 32

SCORING SUMMARY

G	Per	Time	Team	Goal Scorer	Assist	Assist	PHX	DET	STR
1	1	3:39	DET	B. SHANAHAN (24)	P. DATSYUK (21)	K. DRAPER (20)	14 13 55 34 33 15	3 34 33 30 28 19	EV
2	1	10:13	CBJ	R. WHITNEY (19)	G. SANDERSON (23)	A. CASSELS (36)	5 40 34 25 11	14 3 30 29 25 8	PP
3	2	2:02	DET	B. HULL (28)	J. WOOLLEY (18)	P. DATSYUK (22)	17 3 40 34 15 13	7 61 44 30 28 21	EV
4	2	10:19	CBJ	R. KLESLA (1)	R. WHITNEY (45)	M. SILLINGER (23)	3 96 34 21 19 15	44 7 30 29 16 14	EV
5	3	9:39	DET	B. SHANAHAN (25)	J. WOOLLEY (19)	P. DATSYUK (23)	14 5 34 19 15 13	7 34 30 16 14	PP

A Special Tribute to Mr. & Mrs. Ilitch

*Thank you to Mike and Marian Ilitch for 20 years of Detroit Red Wings ownership
and their commitment to hockey excellence
with three Stanley Cup victories in the last seven years!
And, congratulations to Mr. Ilitch
on his induction into the NHL Hockey Hall of Fame this season.*

*The dedication you both have shown to Hockeytown is an amazing testimony
to your love of the game and the city of Detroit.*

Let's Go Red Wings!